good deed rain

Books by Allen Frost

Ohio Trio (Bottom Dog Press 2001)

Bowl of Water (Bottom Dog Press 2003)

Another Life (Bird Dog Publishing 2007)

Home Recordings (Bird Dog Publishing 2009)

The Mermaid Translation (Bird Dog Publishing 2010)

The Selected Correspondence of Kenneth Patchen edited by Allen Frost (Bottom Dog Press 2012)

The Wonderful Stupid Man (Bird Dog Publishing 2012)

Saint Lemonade (Good Deed Rain 2014)

Playground (Good Deed Rain 2014)

Roosevelt (Good Deed Rain 2015)

5 Novels (Good Deed Rain 2015)

The Sylvan Moore Show (Good Deed Rain 2015)

Town in a Cloud (Good Deed Rain 2015)

A Flutter of Birds Passing Through Heaven: A Tribute To Robert Sund edited by Allen Frost and Paul Piper (Good Deed Rain 2016)

At the Edge of America (Good Deed Rain 2016)

Lake Erie Submarine (Good Deed Rain 2016)

LAKE ERIE SUBMARINE
ALLEN FROST

Lake Erie Submarine ©2016 Good Deed Rain
Bellingham, Washington
ISBN 978-1-68419-839-9
Cover Photograph: Brian Smith
Writing, Drawings & Interior Photos: Allen Frost
Photo of d.a. levy's poem "Refrigerator Mantra"
Production Assistance: Fred Sodt
Apple: TFK!

Ohio poems written in Huron, Milan,
        Cleveland, Norwalk, Oberlin

For James Tate & Dome of the Hidden Pavilion

INTRODUCTION

These poems were written during a two week family vacation to Ohio last summer. Every time we visit Ohio, I welcome the inspiration there. This visit was also made eventful by Larry Smith's gift of the latest James Tate book. I got on a real James Tate kick, and these poems probably reflect that. I enjoyed the realization that there were poems lurking all around the sunny neighborhood. The idea for the title poem came to me when I was walking alone along the beach early in the morning. There were footprints in the sand but no sign of who left them. Lake Erie was calm, with the sun low, and I thought of some ancient submarine. The crew would go ashore when no one else was around. Then they disappeared underwater before anybody showed. It's probably been happening since Jules Verne's day. I kept watching for it, but like so many things on this glimpse of Ohio, there are only traces of magic left behind.

Allen Frost
a summer later
Bellingham, Washington

the jetlag
the red kite
the umbrella
the contraption
the lake erie submarine
the ohio birds
the snow
the fox
the airport
the birdwatcher
the ghost
the art
the ships
the horse
the crickets again
the buzzards
the bait shop
the smallest woman in town
the trains
the lightning bug
the lighthouse
the peddler
the sunflowers
the holy water

the silence
the orphans
the drive-in
the compliment
the meteor shower
the better leaf
the tugboats
the fortune teller
the jar
the yawn
the small talk
the layers
the secret button
the task
the last paperboy
the girls

THE JETLAG

Our son has been asleep for seven hours.
I think he's got the jetlag. That's what it is.
From Seattle to Ohio and straight upstairs.
His molecules have been sifted by handfuls
poured into ancient bellows and blown
in slow motion to settle upon the
heated daylight of these green
lazy neighborhood leaves.

once I'm here

THE RED KITE

Once I'm here, surrounded by trees
the first thing I hear above me is a cardinal.
He doesn't travel out west. He stays here
on this side of the country and his song
is a tied red kite.

they made it disappear

THE UMBRELLA

The rumor is true.
They leveled the beautiful overgrown field,
the big old oak, the farm house.
They folded all that up like an umbrella
and they made it disappear.
I hear the man who lived there
held out for as long as he could.
Until finally, with a little more pressure
they folded him up too.

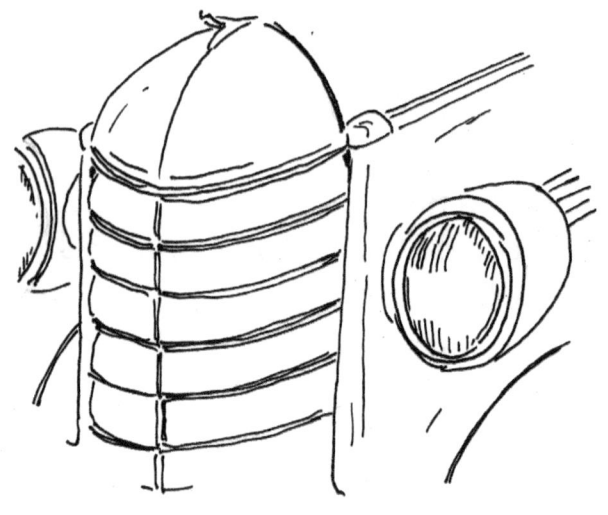

driving by in the night

THE CONTRAPTION

The crickets wait for dark to start
the wheels of their sleep machine.
Out in the grass, the contraption creaks.
The windows are open, a breeze blows,
a train is passing, a moth is driving
by in the night.

wave after wave

THE LAKE ERIE SUBMARINE

Wave after wave comes in
to cover the footprints of the crew
some barefoot, some in shoes

Look along the sand
you can even see
where their dog ran free

gathered at the feeder

THE OHIO BIRDS

Yellow Billed Cuckoo, Acadian Flycatcher,
Eastern Phoebe, Mockingbird, Warbler,
Eastern Bluebird, Scarlet Tanager, Cardinal,
Rose Breasted Grosbeak, Indigo Bunting
and Oriole. I've been admiring Ohio birds
gathered at the feeder and Larry says
I can take some with me when we go home
as long as they fit in one suitcase.

THE SNOW

What happened to all the snow
we heard so much about last winter

Has it gone into hiding
holding to the slats of a picket fence

Under a pine
on the house siding
white as an unwritten page

pacing the wire

THE FOX

No, I don't want to see the fox in the cage.
I know the story—he would have died if
they didn't rescue him and stick him in there.
His leg will never work again, they explain
he could never survive in the wild.
Pacing the wire, ragged coat, teeth
dull as silverware, he's been sprung
from one trap and put in another.

planes flew off

THE AIRPORT

The airport is gone and the 8 year old
tells me they burned it, like you would do
with a hornet nest.
The scared planes flew off down the shore.
The land will become something else again
once the smoke clears.

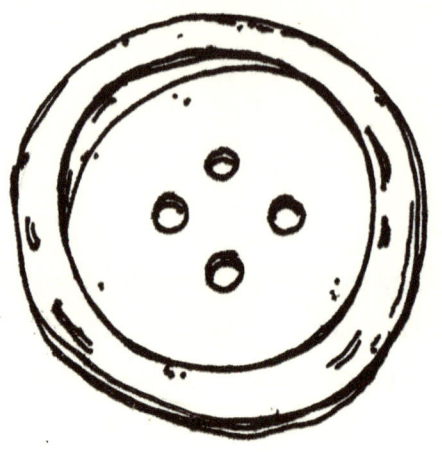

a missing button

THE BIRDWATCHER

At first they didn't notice me. Who cares
if I sit on the porch and watch the birds?
It wasn't until I got binoculars and saw more.
Now they're so close I can see that grackle
hasn't changed his shirt for two days.
There's a wren with a missing button.
A sparrow hasn't tied her shoe.

floating above

THE GHOST

Sure enough, behind the Goodwill there's a ghost. It's not the guy in the blue smock who works there, smoking a cigarette by the green dumpster. He found the perfect spot to take a break. He doesn't even seem aware that isn't smoke floating above him in the air.

facing the parking lot

THE ART

There are three framed pencil drawings for sale
at the grocery store. Custer, Mother Theresa
and Sitting Bull. They've been there for years
on the windowsill facing the parking lot
like portholes watching from a ship.

things have gone missing

THE SHIPS

Everyone in town was excited when
the ships arrived on the horizon.
From a distance they looked so small
like a pair of toys, but they've been here
since winter and things have gone missing :
a sailboat, a footbridge, a row of maple trees
a gas station and two houses on Berlin Road.
Three or four cars disappear every few weeks
and a hundred feet of Mill Street is gone.
It keeps getting worse as the ships
get lower in the water. There are white lines
painted on the bows, so you can keep track.
It seems pretty clear they won't leave
until they have all they came here for.

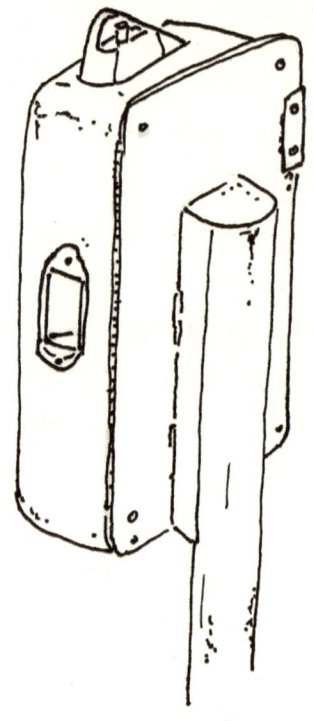

a minute ride

THE HORSE

We drove to the supermarket tonight.
It was about the same as the last time
until I looked for the coin-operated horse.
It only costs a penny for a minute ride,
a shiny plastic saddle with stirrups
a leather rein to hold and a painted smile.
It would hum and roll forward and back.
So what happened to it? Where did it go?
Maybe someone made a mistake and fed it
a quarter and it ran right thru the door.

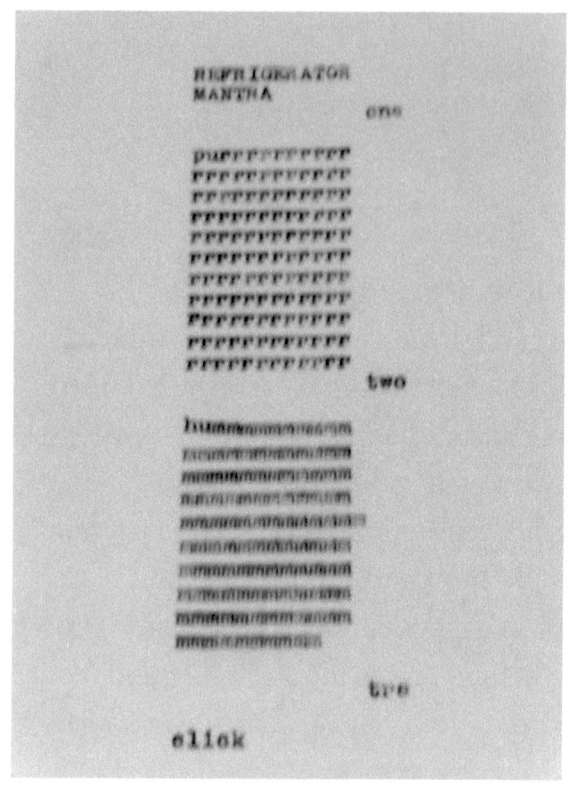

pattern or meaning

THE CRICKETS AGAIN

This time I'm trying really hard to listen to them, to find some sort of pattern or meaning to their sound. I guess I'm trying to break their code. But it's late, the lamp is off, I'm lying in bed, warm, tired, drifting. They have been with us here for a long time and they're good at what they do. With my eyes closed, my mind wanders. Their sound has dimension and depth. I see where they're leading me, it's obvious. I know I'm not the only one to go down this road. I know that sleep is just around the corner.

looking for something

THE BUZZARDS

The way they lurk across the bright blue sky
wearing frayed overcoats, stretched black
sleeves held into the air, you get the feeling
they're looking for something precious to
them. And they are. They cover the land
from yard to yard, along the roads and
over parking lots, hour after hour, day
after day.

in the background

THE BAIT SHOP

There's a Closed sign on the bait shop.
The windows are boarded up.
In the background the lake is still there.
You can follow the dock
and climb the ladder down to the float.
You can touch the water with your hand
and see the little fish schooled below.

nothing uncommon

THE SMALLEST WOMAN IN TOWN

He stood there and watched her.
There was nothing uncommon about him.
He wore a t-shirt, shorts and a dull expression.
Everything around him was built to his size.
He stared at her and you could tell there was
something he was dying to say.

a big door in the air

THE TRAINS

There's a big door in the air.
The trains come out of there.
At first you can hear them calling
from way back inside. You can feel
a rumble. Take a step back, quick!
It's on the way. It will be fast and loud
and many cars long. Fortunately
we've learned to live with them.
We built tracks they stay on.
The rails take them to another door
at the far edge of our town.

landed on a leaf

THE LIGHTNING BUG

The lightning bug landed
on a leaf by the birdfeeder.
I heard it try to get started again.
It was having trouble. I had to go out there
with jumper cables, very small ones, made by
a specialty company in Toledo.

the light went on

THE LIGHTHOUSE

I wanted to see who lives in the lighthouse.
Who turns the beams and pulls the foghorn?
So I walked all the way down the beach
and didn't fall off the sharp breakwater.
It took me an hour to get there and I was tired.
I wanted a lemonade. The door was locked
but there was a sign next to a long white string.
When I pulled it, the light went on.
The foghorn blew. I guess now I knew
I have a job to do.

at your job

THE PEDDLER

He's not someone
you want to see at your door.
He's got things you were hoping to forget.
There are photos of you at your job
the one you'll be returning to soon enough.
But he's got other things for sale too
like that pencil you keep on your desk.
You would like to slam the door in his face
or call the police, but you have to be polite.
Put yourself in his shoes. He's just trying
to make a living.

with the rest of them

THE SUNFLOWERS

Try to be calm, try your best to smile.
If you stand here long enough it will happen
face tilted to the sun, moved only by the wind
turn down all the sound and imagine you're in
a crowd at a station, waiting with the rest of
them for a train that might never come.

so it wouldn't spill

THE HOLY WATER

For ten minutes it rained furiously
as if the Great Lake had been tipped on edge.
Then gradually, all the machinery of town,
connected by pulleys and lines to the tallest
trees and towers, slowly brought the lake
back down so it wouldn't spill away.
The sidewalks were left slick with puddles
the parked cars shined and all the rainspouts
poured like church organs.

filled with the sound

THE SILENCE

In the driveway, a yellow sign is nailed to
a tree: *Deaf Person*. Telegraph Road is loud
with rushing cars. They are little worlds filled
with the sound of radios and conversations
and kids saying, "Are we there yet?"
But whoever lives inside that house
goes by in silence.

out of the crop

THE ORPHANS

It's another dark middle of the night
and the orphans come out of the crop.
The corn stalks know the routine
they whisper and hush and sigh
as the orphans pass through
to surround the parked car.
When those teenagers come back
from the black ruins of the orphanage
after they've given up looking for ghosts
that aren't there, won't they be surprised
to find little handprints all over their
windows and doors?

in another world

THE DRIVE-IN

Go to the Star View Drive-In tonight.
You could stop at the booth and pay $8
to see some new Hollywood blur, or
if you prefer, try the next lane over…
A green splash of headlights as you dip
from the asphalt into a secret ravine.
Like a wheelbarrow pushing into the tall grass
snapping stalks, the trailing vines of creeper
and wildflowers, the rush and crush of weeds.
For a moment you'll be in dark shadow
the blink it takes to pop up in another world.
When you steer out of that, you're holding
the wheel of a 1957 Chevrolet and you are
in a big field full of other old cars like yours
parked in chrome rows and you've never seen
a screen so filled with Technicolor.

the compliment

THE COMPLIMENT

Calvin says she looks cute
in those shorts and striped shirt
green and pink as watermelon.
He also likes her laugh.
He even gives her a dollar
but her mother makes her
give it back.

THE METEOR SHOWER

Waiting for the sky, it takes a while for that
hot bright day painted up there to fade and
cool. Shadows start to emerge across the yard,
lightning bugs fly low enough to catch.
Bats unstring lanterns overhead, the first stars
appear. Another hour has to pass, mosquito
repellant goes on. You need a chair to lean
back in, or just stand and stare.
At first you doubt whether you saw anything
between outer space and the blinking lights
of passing airplanes. A quick scratch goes by.
The trees whisper. A cricket startles you,
creeping over your foot. A creature snaps
a twig in the woods, yellow eyes look back.

It's okay, it's just the neighbor's cat walking
along the property line. The sky shows more
stars. How deep a puddle are we in? A meteor
drives past with a sparking tail of tin cans.
There's no telling how long it takes for the
next one. When it happens, it looks big as
a city bus on fire. It's so bright and marvelous
you can watch the trail of confetti thrown out
windows before it vanishes against our
atmosphere on the edge of our planet
and all that we hold dear.

into the forest

THE BETTER LEAF

Before I could stop him, he killed the moth.
He stepped on it and said he hated them and
there was a snap between its brown wings
as it died. I put a flat stone over it with a
leaf I called a flower. He said, "That's not a
flower!" and he ran off into the forest
between the elephant legs of oak and maple
past where we saw the frog living in the
hollow. There aren't any flowers I can see
just dirt and scuffs of grass, branches and dry
leaves, but he leaned down and said he found
one. Sometimes they drop from the treetops
after their whole life in the breeze, sun and
moonbeams. When they die it takes a very
keen eye to spot them fallen and soft as a
feather and much better than a leaf.

we must be adrift

THE TUGBOATS

After last night's rain, it doesn't seem possible
there could be any land. We must be adrift
in ten feet of water and tugboats are needed
to rope the neighborhood together again.

one sunny day

THE FORTUNE TELLER

"Oh yes," she says. "You can come back as a
bird. You can sing all day and fly from tree to
tree and everything you need is free. So many
of the things that weigh you down in in this
life will be gone. They won't even occur to
you. Your short life as a bird will repeat
doing the same thing over and over
and then one sunny day, you might wonder.
From your perch on a branch
in the middle of your song you will stop
at the clear bell of a memory."

THE JAR

With a house full of kids and grandkids
it gets so noisy, and I had to get away to find
some quiet. I went outside and put my ear to
a rose of Sharon flower and listened to that
soft cone. A cicada buzzed and rested and
started again. I borrowed a bicycle and went
for a ride. I went down a street bordered and
shadowed by tall oak trees. I rode on the tar
and the fat tires hummed. There was a kid
up ahead selling something in jars.
Lemonade, I guessed. It was hot so I stopped.
"How much for the lemonade" I asked.

He was about ten. He got a look on his face
and told me, "It's not lemonade."
I looked closer at the row of jars on the table.
He was right. They looked empty. He held
one up. "This one's the sound of a train."
He tapped the next, "This is an ice cream
truck. And this here's a police car I heard
last night." I said, "Oh gee, I was hoping for
something nice and quiet." He said, "Here,"
and passed me a little clear jelly jar.
"What is it?" I asked him.
"It's empty," he said.

nothing to do

THE YAWN

I was sitting outside on a chair in the sun.
Just when I yawned, a hummingbird dived
and snatched that breath from me. I saw it
rush and it was gone to another yard.
That's okay. I don't need that yawn.
It's a warm afternoon, I've got nothing to do
I think I can find another one.

in your sleep

THE SMALL TALK

Trying to make small talk with a 10 year old
I said the first thing that popped into my head
"Do you still walk in your sleep?"
"Not anymore," she said.

the tall cliff

THE LAYERS

The Vermilion River is lined with thin slate
gray slices like the shingles on a dragon.
I picked one up and felt the weight and shape
in my hand. When I threw it at the stream
it skipped across the water more times than I
could count and clacked against the tall cliff
on the other shore.
I'm down in the skeleton of the old quarry
where you can read the layers of rock.
Martian colors of rust and brown and time
can be counted uphill from that spot.
Near the top you can see the familiar
reminders of the last century: a locomotive
buried with its rails, coffee pots, bedsprings
car parts, a dented mailbox caught in the press
and a lawnmower sprouts where someone
once came too close to the drop.
The world doesn't stop adding layers
whatever has been, even today's sunshine
leaves its dust on the land.

that old worry

THE SECRET BUTTON

Only when things get calm, when it's night
and the window is open to the crickets
you listen to that old worry that tells you
time is running out. Vacation is almost over
and it won't be long until school starts again.
You know it can't be stopped, but is there
a way to slow it down? Try to trick time
lure it back like a cat? Stay up late, pay no
attention to clocks, or calendars, or routines.
Maybe it's cleverly hidden, maybe there's
a button hidden in a tree you can press
but in all these years of looking
I haven't found it yet.

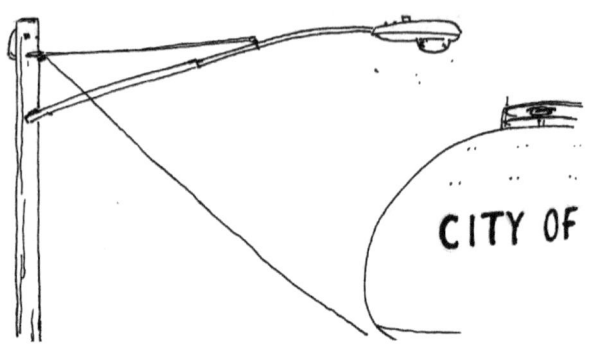

what they're making

THE TASK

Every night I hear the crickets out there
sawing away, busy gluing something together
in the glowing streetlamps. They seem very
proud of what they're making and why not?
It's an amazing house, built to the exact
proportions of one of the old mansions
you see along the lake. I'm a little surprised
they're so good at the task, but they've had
years to practice, haven't they? And then
the train comes through. You hear the engine
rumble and the horn and the roar on the rails
blows at their creation and pieces of it scatter
across the lawns and gardens. When the train
passes, the crickets haven't stopped.
They just go right on with their
repairs and reconstruction.

like a rare bird

THE LAST PAPERBOY

He walks in the rain, head bent down,
with two shoulder bags full of newspapers.
Honestly, I didn't even know his kind still
existed. He goes about his job like a rare bird,
crossing the wet street, under the awnings and
fire escapes, trying a locked door with hands
black from newsprint. We had to stop the car
recklessly beside the curb to capture him in a
photograph.

THE GIRLS

When he was nearly 13, he used to drive a horse carriage through the town. Of course there were cars by then and a horse on the street wasn't unusual. But it was the end of an era. As if they were well aware, there were two girls who would wait on the sidewalk to ride with him. Wearing their finest clothes, long dresses and hats they would climb onto the wooden seat behind him and ride from West Main to the wooded edge of town.

Lake Erie Submarine
written in Ohio from 8/6/15—8/19/15

www.ingramcontent.com/pod-product-compliance
Lightning Source LLC
Chambersburg PA
CBHW060538080526
44586CB00012B/784